AF095240

OPERATION EVASION

"The Ghost In You"

BESTSELLING AUTHOR

PETE THRON

To Paul and Dorothy Roche (Tobias's parents). There is a right and thoughtful way to go ahead in life. Always show respect to those who have earned it. Be good to your friends and always punish your enemies!

This story is inspired by the actual events that occurred during the case of Operation Evasion, the largest passenger cocaine smuggling investigation at Miami Airport. It features Tobias Roche the federal agent and Evelyn Bozon Papa the Columbian Fem-Fatale. The fictitious characters of this book are not intended to refer to any actual persons and any similarity is unintended and entirely coincidental.

Preface

Tobias Roche has often been asked "What has been the most important investigative case that he has worked on over the past 50 years?" Roche has been a Police Officer, Deputy U.S. Marshal, Chief Deputy U.S. Marshal, Special Agent, Supervisory Special Agent, U.S. Government Contractor, and Licensed Private Investigator.

He continues to work in the criminal justice investigative field to this day. Toby is the first federal agent that I have ever written about, and his unique personality, diligence to detail, and always working towards resolution are second to none. Let's not sugarcoat it, Roche is the kind of guy this country doesn't make anymore. A dinosaur with a badge and a memory sharper than a switchblade.

He came up hard, made mistakes, pissed off more than a few brass, and still walked the walk every damn day. He's not here for the trophies. He's not here for the press conferences. He's here for *closure*. And if you're dirty, if you're lying, if you're on the run, you better believe he's coming. It might take him years. It might take him decades. But he's coming.

I've written about many cops, but Toby? He's different. He's not the kind of guy who talks about "public service" in press kits. He's the kind who still knows the sound of a pager going off in a motel at 3 a.m. What it feels like when a CI gets clipped because someone gets sloppy. He's been in the thick of It since polyester uniforms and revolvers were standard issue.

You don't build a résumé like Roche's by waiting around in squad rooms. You build it by knocking on doors, sitting on wiretaps, flipping witnesses, and going where the dirt lives.

And he's done it across every alphabet soup agency you can name, Marshals, Customs, ATF, Secret Service, and everything in between. He answers the question with a unique perspective.

Tobias is known for being the author, developer, and coordinator of Operation Flagship with the U.S. Marshals Service. While being the youngest Chief Deputy U.S. Marshal in modern times (29 years of age,) and managing the District of Colombia office under his former boss and lifetime friend Herb Rutherford.

The fugitive sting operation yielded over 150 arrests in a little over 3 hours in one location. The unsuspecting fugitives were offered free tickets to a Washington Redskins football game, on a Sunday afternoon in December of 1985. It is legendary in law enforcement circles and is proudly displayed in the U.S. Marshals Museum.

That operation was balls-to-the-wall brilliance. Most people don't realize the size of that con. It wasn't just flyers and fake tickets. It was months of prep, layers of logistics, actors, decoys, scripts, and a whole lot of praying nobody caught wise before showtime. You've got to be part street hustler and part tactician to pull something like that off.

Roche wasn't some figurehead in a suit pointing at a whiteboard. He was writing scripts, mapping out escape routes, choosing music playlists to keep the perps calm before the cuffs dropped. That day in D.C., he stood in front of the dais, headset on, counting takedowns in real time like an orchestra conductor.

And when those gates closed behind the 150-plus dirtbags, some of them killers, he didn't even celebrate. Just nodded, turned off his mic, and said, "Next case."

That's Toby. Always ten steps ahead. No time to dwell. No room for ego. This innovative idea (created by Roche) has been the topic of documentaries on ESPN and NFL films.

It also served as the specific inspiration for the 2024 suspenseful hit movie "Trap" by Producer/Director M. Night Shyamalan. Tobias, always a risk taker and overachiever, has always displayed professionalism in his law enforcement career. He values loyalty to those who work hard and develop self-initiated investigations.

Let's be clear, Toby never played politics. If you were a worker, he would have your back. If you were out grinding at 5 a.m. with stale coffee in your gut and five warrants in your vest, you were family.

But if you were one of the frauds, one of those spineless opportunists who coasted off someone else's hustle, he'd smell you a mile off.

He's not polite about it, either. There's a fire behind his eyes when he talks about the leeches in the system. The paper-pushers who never made a collar but talk like they wrote the Bible on criminal investigation. He kept his loyalty tight. Earned, not handed out. You get one shot with Toby. Blow it, and you're done.

Roche despises "Butt Snorkelers," who live off others work with no significant investigative experience. They just kiss ass 24/7 to get ahead. He also hates "Ride Along's" those who hang out in the office with the hope of going on a search warrant, arrest, or seizure of someone else's case.

This scum then claims it as their work on promotional exams. We all know these types of people in our profession.

You've seen these clowns. They hang back in the office till the radios light up, then magically appear at the scene like they did something. First ones to post on LinkedIn. First to hand in a résumé. But when the shots are fired, or the CI goes missing? They're nowhere.

Roche called them out, publicly, loudly. Didn't matter if they wore stripes or had friends at HQ. He lit'em up. Told one guy during a staff meeting, "You don't work cases. You collect coffee cups."

That's Toby, zero filter. A throwback to when the badge meant work, not likes.

Tobias says however, that the most life changing event for him in the criminal justice system occurred in 1993 and 2021.

It involved him and his former nemesis, Evelyn Bozon Papa. Bozon Papa was a Colombian national who was known as the "The Femme Fatale" to the narcotics agents. She helped orchestrate a powerful organization within the Cali Cartel in Miami. The events surrounding Roche's investigation and outcome took over 30 years.

He never forgot her. Evelyn Bozon Papa. Back in 'ninety-three, she was fire in a bottle, smart, calculating, seductive, and lethal in the dope world. She moved multi-kilos of cocaine for the Cali Cartel and bodies were left by her associates. Everyone wanted her. DEA, FBI, and Interpol. But it was Roche who got her.

He worked her case as a surgeon would when operating on a patient. Careful, clean, and methodical. Roche dug through mountains of intelligence, flipped her associates, leaned on airline insiders, and pulled it all together like a puzzle from hell. When the indictment hit, she didn't stand a chance.

But here's where it gets twisted. Decades later, that same woman's daughter reached out. And instead of brushing her off, Toby listened. Because time had done something neither badge nor bars could, it humbled her. And it changed him. Toby was a middle-class kid who went to an all-white high school, while Evelyn was a farm girl from Colombia. Their paths crossed in the world in which they were involved.

This is a powerful story of how two individuals with different and diverse backgrounds collided with each other. The characters on both sides created an environment of intrigue and suspense. The twists and turns in the law enforcement and criminal justice system are fully displayed in this book. There is a shocking conclusion to the circle of events!

It's rare for a fed to look at a former target and say, "Yeah, we're both different people now." But that's exactly what Toby did. He flew to Colombia. Met Evelyn's family. Ate meals in homes where his name used to be a curse. That's not weak. That's guts.

This case, their case, wasn't just paperwork. It was personal. And it stretched over continents, decades, prison walls, and broken hearts. It's the kind of story Hollywood tries to write but always gets wrong. Except this time, they didn't. When I pressed Toby to answer the question "What is the most important investigative case that you worked on in the last 50 years?"

Roche answered by saying, "It is now Operation Evasion, as it took over 30 years to reach a successful conclusion!"

This unique scenario, between Toby and Evelyn, was documented by Univision and nominated for a Latin Emmy Award in 2024. The story continues today and in the future.

"Operation Evasion." It's not just a case name. It's a time capsule. A personal monument to what it takes to close a loop that should've never stayed open.

Over 30 years, dozens of players, and one relentless son of a bitch who refused to forget.

Roche could've let it rot in the archives. Could've said, "Not my problem anymore." But that's not him. He hunted it down until the last thread was tied off. Until Bozon Papa walked out into the light. Until justice wasn't just a word, it was a fact. And here we are, decades later, and the story's still breathing. *Still alive. Still*

Chapter I

The Legacy of Tobias Roche: A Law Enforcement Icon:

Tobias Roche is the first federal agent I have written about, and without a doubt, one of the most fascinating individuals I have ever encountered. His law enforcement career spans nearly five decades, a tenure filled with high-stakes operations, legendary arrests, and unwavering dedication to criminal justice. To say his career has been interesting would be a massive understatement.

The Man Behind the Badge:

Before delving into his background and achievements, it's essential to understand the character of Tobias Roche. Known to his colleagues as "Toby," he values honesty and loyalty above all else. These principles have earned him the trust of everyone he has worked with—as a police officer, deputy, inspector, and Chief Deputy with the U.S. Marshals Service; as a special agent, senior special agent, and supervisory special agent with the U.S. Customs Service; and later as a supervisory special agent with U.S. Immigration and Customs Enforcement.

Today, Toby continues to serve as a consultant to various federal agencies, offering expertise on high-profile law enforcement and intelligence missions, including then U.S. Senator Marco Rubio (R/Florida), now U.S. Secretary of State on, Venezuela matters. He remains a valuable resource, referring to active and complex investigations, while maintaining an extensive network of confidential informants which led to the indictments of the top international fugitives from Venezuela.

Despite his formidable career, Tobias Roche is still, at heart, a small-town kid from Western Massachusetts. Proud of his middle-class upbringing, he frequently returns to honor his roots, pay homage to his late parents, and reunite with old friends over drinks at local bars.

He fondly recalls his youth, with some of his best memories tied to summers spent working as a lifeguard. Toby always tries to treat everyone fairly, regardless of race, ethnicity, gender, or social status, and is always ready to lend a hand. During his years in law enforcement, he has also run into people who tried to take advantage of his hard-earned work.

I have experienced that as a cop, and it's very irritating to say the least.

Over the years, he has experienced the diversity of America firsthand, embracing the laid-back culture of Western Massachusetts, partying in Atlanta, navigating the distinct dynamics of Los Angeles, and Washington D.C. Ultimately making his home in bilingual Miami.

Though he grew up in liberal Massachusetts, Toby identifies as a conservative Republican, fitting seamlessly into his Kendall neighborhood in Miami. He often jokes that, as a Caucasian male over sixty-five in Miami-Dade County, he is now a minority. However, one thing is still clear; he is a fiercely loyal friend to those he holds dear but has no tolerance for disloyalty or deceit. His disdain for individuals who take credit for others' hard work is well known. In his signature blunt style, he refers to such opportunists as "Butt Boys" and, in Florida, escalates the term to "Butt Snorkeling Assholes."

A Career Built on Valor and Integrity:

Toby's career is defined by action, courage, and a no-nonsense approach to criminal justice. He has always had little patience for career climbers who lack field experience, those who have made fewer than five arrests, have never been in a life-threatening altercation, yet somehow rise through the ranks. He loathes those who bring donuts to the office to win favor with superiors while avoiding the real dangers of the job.

To Toby, respect in law enforcement is earned in the field, not in the break room.

He acknowledges that many law enforcement officers he has worked with 95% are of the highest caliber. He has always appreciated supervisors who lead by example and has fiercely defended agents unfairly targeted by upper management. Whether standing up for minorities facing discrimination or protecting officers from bureaucratic retaliation, Tobias Roche has been a champion for equality within law enforcement. *A Decorated and*

Accomplished Lawman:

Toby's law enforcement journey began in earnest in the 1970s. A former grade school student, hall monitor wielded his principal-granted badge with authority. He went on to earn degrees in criminal justice from Holyoke Community College (A, S,), Westfield State College (B.S.) and American International College (M.S.) and Ph.D., criminology instruction, achieving high academic honors at every level.

As an athlete, he was equally impressive, winning two bronze medals in the USA Masters National Swimming Championship, placing third in the USA National Duathlon and Triathlon Championships, and completing the grueling 28.8-mile Manhattan NYC Swim Race and the Boston Marathon—twice.

From Small-Town Cop to Elite Federal Agent:

In 1975, Tobias worked as a Law Enforcement Assistance Administration police intern with the U.S. Department of Justice. He then joined the Amherst,

Massachusetts Police Department as a Community Service Officer, handling police duties without carrying a weapon.

By 1977, he was a full-fledged police officer in Wilbraham, Massachusetts, making hundreds of arrests and earning numerous commendations. However, Toby craved more action. He set his sights on federal law enforcement, drawn to the reputation and integrity of the U.S. Marshals Service. In 1980, he became a Deputy U.S. Marshal, tracking down fugitives in Atlanta. His first major case? The hunt for Christopher Boyce, the infamous spy from *The Falcon and the Snowman*.

During his tenure in Atlanta, he was stabbed by a Cuban Mariel inmate inside the Bureau of Prisons' Atlanta facility. With characteristic grit, Tobias disarmed the attacker, breaking the convict's arm in two separate places. His bravery earned him a written citation from the U.S. Department of Justice.

Mastering the Art of Manhunting:

By 1984, Toby had proven himself as an exceptional fugitive investigator. He was promoted to Inspector in Los Angeles and later led the famous FIST VII operation in Hartford, Connecticut, a sting operation that remains legendary. The Hartford team had an astonishing arrest rate of 104 fugitives per team over eight weeks, setting a record that still stands today. "**Boy George Sting**" which invited fugitives to breakfast with the group and free concert tickets.

His most famous ruse/sting, however, was **Operation Flagship** in 1985, a covert operation in Washington, D.C. that led to the single largest fugitive multiple arrests in law enforcement history, with over 150 arrests in one operation. The case was later featured on *ESPN 30/30, NFL Films*, and *Wikipedia*. **It was the inspiration for the hit movie "Trap" released in 2024.**

Transition to U.S. Customs and Homeland Security:

In 1988, Tobias transferred to U.S. Customs in Miami, tackling fraud, narcotics, and money laundering cases for over a decade. By 1999, he was a Supervisory Special Agent, leading the nation's top asset forfeiture unit and co-founding what is now known as the *Kleptocracy* initiative, targeting foreign political corruption. More awards for Toby and his gang! Following the 9/11 attacks, he volunteered for body recovery at Ground Zero, an experience that left him with severe medical issues, although he never complains.

Post-Retirement and Continued Service:

Retirement wasn't the end of the road. From 2006 to 2010, Toby worked as a contract national program manager with DHS's National Firearms and Tactical Training Unit. Later, he also held contracts with ATF and the U.S. Secret Service, investigating international money laundering and asset forfeiture cases. In 2021-2023, he was appointed by Governor Ron DeSantis and served as a Commissioner with the Florida Athletic Commission for Boxing and Combat Sports.

From 2022-2023, he served as an NHL Security Representative in Florida. Childhood dreams for Toby!

The Legend Continues:

Today, Tobias Roche stays deeply involved in the war on crime, using his extensive global network to gather intelligence on some of the world's most dangerous criminals. His story is one of resilience, courage, and relentless pursuit of justice. Toby is a loving father and loyal friend who always has your back. From small-town Massachusetts kid to high-stakes federal agent, to hunting fugitives and shaping international criminal investigation policy, Tobias Roche's legacy is etched in the annals of law enforcement history.

And this is only the beginning of an important law enforcement investigation full of twists and multiple challenges.

Chapter II

Evelyn Bozon Pappa, was born on June 10, 1961, in a small, tightly knit Colombian community where tradition and patriarchy shaped much of her daily life. From an early age, Evelyn's life was marked by challenges that would have broken many. Yet, somehow, she endured.

Her early childhood was modest, spent among rolling hills and dusty roads, in a neighborhood where everyone knew each other's names. Her parents were hardworking, humble people. Her father was a laborer who worked long days under the relentless sun, and her mother, a homemaker whose life revolved around her children and her faith. Evelyn's family didn't have much in the way of material wealth, but they held fast to their religious convictions and cultural customs. She was raised in a deeply religious household that, while providing a sense of spiritual grounding, also reinforced a rigidly traditional view of gender roles. In that environment, girls were expected to be obedient, nurturing, and compliant, often sacrificing their desires for the sake of the family and especially for the men in their lives.

Evelyn learned from an early age to keep her voice down, to walk behind rather than besides, and to say yes even when every personal instinct screamed no. Tragically, at the tender age of eleven, Evelyn's innocence was shattered when a family member sexually abused her. This violation was a painful secret she would carry in silence for years, weighed down by cultural shame and the fear of not being believed. In a community where family honor was sacred, speaking out was unthinkable. The emotional weight of that experience marked the beginning of a lifetime of trauma.

This early trauma set the tone for a life of submission and endurance, where her sense of agency was gradually stripped away. Her identity, her dreams, and her sense of self-worth were slowly dismantled by the abuse and the social silence that followed. There was no justice. No comfort. No protection. Just the expectation that she would move on and behave as though nothing had happened.

By the time she was fourteen, Evelyn was forced into a marriage with Carlos Romero Paez, a much older man whose charisma masked a deeply violent and controlling nature. Romero Paez, was entrenched deeply in the Colombian drug trade and even served as a narcotics smuggling kingpin for the infamous, deceased drug lord Pablo Escobar. He saw Evelyn not only as a partner, but also as property, a woman to control, use, and silence.

From the outset, their marriage was marked by psychological manipulation, physical abuse, sexual abuse, and emotional isolation. Evelyn was no longer a girl with dreams, but due to Romero Paez, was recruited into the drug smuggling world.

He would strike her for questioning him, forbid her from seeing friends and family, and regularly accuse her of disloyalty. Her world shrank until it consisted only around Romero

Paez, their home, and the secret she kept hidden behind closed doors. Evelyn became trapped in a cycle of violence, control, and dependency.

She bore his children, endured his wrath, and prayed to a God she often wondered had forgotten her. Ms. Bozon Papa chose the dark side. Carlos Romero Paez was not just any man. He was a key figure in the international cocaine trade and, more chillingly, one of Pablo Escobar's helicopter pilots.

He ferried massive quantities of cocaine kilos and weapons across borders, evading law enforcement with the same ease he used to manipulate and control those around him. He wielded money and fear with equal precision.

He would brag about his connections and intimidate anyone who questioned his authority. He ordered the deaths of those who stood against him.

He later became a key figure in the Cali Cartel and was associated with the Rodriguez brothers. At home, Romero was a dictator. He dictated every aspect of Evelyn's life, from where she went to what she said, how she dressed, and even how she parented their four children. Evelyn was not a free woman. She lived under his continued abuse.

Even her moments of joy were filtered through his approval. Smiles were fleeting and peace was rare. Evelyn became a key participant in Romero's criminal narcotics smuggling enterprise.

She was careful to never touch the drugs herself, but she coordinated the covert operations happening around her domain.

Her home became a sanctuary for drug traffickers, corrupt relatives, and a hub of illegal dealings, Bozon Papa would later learn to wield her own power as a leader of the narcotic operations through Romero, who had expanded his operation into The United States.

That smuggling venture (Operation Evasion) was based at the Miami International Airport, where Evelyn became "The Fem Fatale." At the age of thirty-four, Evelyn's life changed irrevocably. She was indicted by federal authorities in the United States for conspiracy to distribute cocaine.

The charges were severe and had devastating consequences. Unlike Romero, who immediately fled to Colombia to avoid arrest, Evelyn did not run. When she reported to U.S. federal courthouse (Miami) relative to a federal grand jury subpoena, she learned of the formal accusation, and was immediately arrested. Federal prosecutors made it clear that they were willing to negotiate. However, Bozon-Papa refused and decided to take her chances.

She was represented by Cali Cartel lawyers who never had her best interests at heart. Evelyn was falsely told by her corrupt lawyers that she could use the battered wife defense, but the government prosecutors advised her counsel that such defense was inadmissible in federal cases.

Before her trial, Evelyn was assessed several times by professionals who uncovered the depth of her trauma. They learned about the childhood sexual abuse, the forced marriage, the years of manipulation and battery, and the psychological warfare waged against her by Romero Paez. The criminal justice system saw her as a conspirator in one of the largest drug enterprises in history.

Despite this context, Evelyn was found guilty and sentenced to two consecutive life sentences without the possibility of parole, a punishment as extreme as it ensured she would die in prison. She became the first female drug kingpin to receive such a sentence.

The courtroom saw her as complicit and a willing participant, not as someone caught in the grip of a brutal and controlling partner. Romero Paez, for his part, was never brought to justice.

He lived in Colombia for many years after the indictment, beyond the reach of U.S. authorities. Eventually, his violent world caught up with him. He was assassinated in Colombia under circumstances that remain murky, by rivals or former associates in the drug trade. In death as in life, Romero escaped accountability. Incarcerated and isolated from the world she once knew, Evelyn could have succumbed to despair. But instead, she transformed.

Over the course of nearly 30 years in federal prison, Evelyn Bozon Papa evolved from a voiceless victim into a beacon of hope and strength for others. Evelyn had never received an incident report in her decades behind bars, a rare and commendable feat in the prison system. She immersed herself in service, finding purpose in faith and education. She began working in the prison chapel, translating the chaplain's sermons from English to Spanish so that Spanish-speaking inmates could receive spiritual nourishment.

Her linguistic abilities became a bridge for others. Evelyn's days in prison were filled with purpose. From sunrise to sunset, she dedicated herself to improving the lives of those around her.

She became a counselor to women struggling with the weight of their sentences, a surrogate mother to the young and frightened, and a mediator during conflicts.

In a world designed to break people, Evelyn helped build them back up. A testament to Evelyn's impact is the unwavering support she has received from those who worked within the prison system. Eight prison employees have written letters requesting her release, praising her character, transformation, and dedication.

Two former prison guards offered to be interviewed and to publicly advocate for her sentence to be commuted by the President of the United States. Beyond prison walls, Evelyn remains a mother back in Barranquilla.

The four children she brought into the world with Romero Paez bore the scars of their chaotic upbringing. One of her daughters was also a victim of Romero's abuse, a dark legacy that left deep emotional wounds. But in the face of such adversity, Evelyn's children rose above.

All of them have graduated from either college or technical school. They are now contributing to members of society, raising families of their own, and carrying forward the resilience they inherited from their mother. Evelyn's story is more than a cautionary tale. It is a profound narrative of survival, transformation, and the enduring human spirit. She was born into a world that taught her to be silent, to obey, and to endure. She was thrust into the darkness of abuse, exploitation, and criminality. Yet even in the bleakest of places, Evelyn found a way to reclaim her voice, her dignity, and her purpose.

Her life stands as a powerful argument for mercy, for rehabilitation, and for a more compassionate justice system. Evelyn Bozon Pappa is not the same person who was sentenced to die in prison. She is a survivor, a teacher, a mother, a leader, and a woman who has turned pain into purpose.

From an international drug smuggling kingpin, who coordinated massive loads of cocaine to a remorseful person who acknowledges her wrongdoings to humanity. See how these two worlds collided with each other in 1993 and again in 2021.

The federal agent chasing the suspect and securing a conviction, and the remorseful person who made a change. Justice Then and Justice Now!

Chapter III

It was a normal spring day in 1993, the kind of warm and humid afternoon typical of Miami, Florida. Tobias Roche was working as a Senior Special Agent (SSA) with the U.S. Customs Service (USCS), assigned to the Vice-Presidential Florida DEA/Customs Task Group, also known as the FJTG. This prestigious joint operation had been formed back in 1981 by then-Vice President George H.W. Bush, to aggressively combat the influx of narcotics smuggling during the height of the South Florida drug war.

Over the years, the FJTG had evolved into an elite unit consisting of roughly 75 to 100 professionals, special agents, intelligence research specialists, and analysts, all working shoulder to shoulder, to protect the United States. Their mission was multifaceted: coordinate arrests, conduct controlled deliveries of narcotics, and closely collaborate with the U.S. Attorney's Office for the Southern District of Florida, to build airtight criminal cases resulting in indictments and high-stakes forfeitures.

The task force was a unique blend of personnel. On one side, there were the newly minted DEA agents, often referred to as the "Newbies." On the other side, seasoned Customs agents, sometimes cynically labeled the "Castaways," brought years of street-hardened experience. Together, they formed a powerful, symbiotic unit. It was a potent mix of youthful energy and career wisdom.

They were a tightly knit team bound by duty, danger, and a sense of camaraderie that for many of them still exist to this day.

One of the key operational advantages of the FJTG was the dual authority granted to its agents. Each member held Title 21 narcotics investigative authority (via DEA) and border search authority (through Customs). This cross-designation allowed FJTG agents to pursue international drug trafficking operations with unprecedented flexibility.

They could legally follow narcotics across borders and, critically, search without warrants—so long as the drugs remained in plain sight. And so, with that foundation in place, we begin.

On that day, Toby was walking across the street toward the U.S. Customs Service/SAC Miami Office. His destination? A senior manager's inbox. He was submitting a formal grievance, an act that would soon alter the trajectory of his career.

The grievance stemmed from what he saw as the blatant favoritism and willful selection of an underqualified candidate for a prestigious national promotional program. Tobias had dared to challenge the system, and in retaliation, he was transferred to the FJTG. At the time, the atmosphere within the U.S. Customs SAC Miami was toxic. A hostile work environment had been allowed to fester.

Fueled by two senior managers who insulated themselves with a clique of "butt-snorkeling agents" and "ride-along wannabe investigators." Yet, as fate would have it, that retaliatory transfer to the FJTG would prove to be one of the most pivotal and serendipitous turns of Roche's life. Not only would it place him in the middle of high-stakes narcotics and money laundering investigations, but it would also forge lifelong friendships and eventually reveal deep betrayals that would haunt him for years to come.

Toby had just dropped the grievance paperwork off when his cell phone rang. It was a quick call; he needed to return to the FJTG office immediately. Toby put a yellow sticker and drew a happy face on top of the file! Upon his arrival, Tobias was met by Group Supervisor James Williams from the DEA and the FJTG's Co-Director Eddie Medeiros of Customs.

The two men got straight to the point. "We got something," Williams said, flipping a file onto the table. "Courier just landed from Colombia. Avianca Airlines. He's sitting on fifty pounds. Could be a setup for a controlled delivery."

Toby raised an eyebrow. "Is he talking?"

"He's nervous, but he knows the stakes," Medeiros added. "We might have a shot at flipping him. We want you and Kelling to take point."

As the backup supervisor for Group 15, Toby understood the urgency. A controlled delivery meant federal agents would allow the narcotics to reach their destination under surveillance—an intricate operation requiring speed, coordination, and absolute discretion.

Without hesitation, Toby grabbed his partner, DEA Special Agent Mark Kelling.

"Let's roll," Toby muttered, already moving toward the door. Mark caught up, grabbing his keys. "Think he's real or just scared shitless?"

"Doesn't matter. If he leads us to the next tier, we win."

They raced to Miami International Airport, heading straight for the Customs Enclosure. There, they met Customs Inspectors Jay McNamara and Michael Burns. The two inspectors had just interdicted a courier who had flown in from Colombia aboard Avianca Airlines, along with a suitcase carrying fifty pounds of cocaine.

With the help of a Spanish-speaking translator, Roche and Kelling began interviewing the suspect. The man, who we'll refer to as "Allie," agreed to speak.

"You guys don't understand," Allie said in a clipped, irritated voice. "I was told to meet someone. An airline guy. He'd be wearing a red scarf or something. I was supposed to wipe my forehead with another red scarf, the same way he did. That was the signal."

Toby leaned in, his tone calm but firm. "Look, Allie. Fifty pounds of coke means you're looking at mandatory life. But you cooperate and genuinely help us, then maybe I can sell that to the U.S. Attorney."

Allie blinked rapidly, his confidence cracking. "If I talk, they'll kill me. You know that, right?"

"Then help us stop them."

Mark Kelling nodded. "You help us today; you don't walk alone. We make sure of that."

Allie exhaled sharply, the tension in his body slowly unwinding. "Okay. All right."

According to him, after deplaning he was supposed to head toward the customs declaration area and look for an airline employee rubbing a red handkerchief across his forehead. Allie was to mirror the gesture, confirming the identification.

Once contact was made, the employee would take an elevator, past the Concourse E domestic security post, and use a special elevator key, known as the "F Key." Armed with this information, the agents sprang into action.

The four-man team exited the customs enclosure and began canvassing the concourse for the mystery airline employee. Roughly ten minutes later, Inspector McNamara spotted a nervous individual loitering near the elevator, an area strictly reserved for employee access.

"He's twitchy," McNamara muttered. "Let's move on him," Burns replied, stepping forward.

"Sir, you work here?" McNamara asked.

"Yeah, uh, waiting for my cousin," the man stammered. His badge was real but sweat clung to his temples.

"Mind coming with us? Just a few questions," Burns said, his tone polite but firm.

Back inside the Customs Enclosure, Ronnie, as they dubbed him; couldn't keep his story straight.

"So, your cousin's arriving on a flight that doesn't land until tonight?" Toby asked, arms folded.

Ronnie swallowed. "I thought it was earlier. I got the times mixed up."

"Funny," Mark said, leaning forward, "because we have someone who says you're involved. Now, we can do this the hard way, or you can start explaining."

Ronnie looked between the agents, then dropped his head.

"I didn't sign up for this," he whispered. "They said I would just open a door."

Toby slid a Miranda waiver and consent-to-search form in front of him. After reading Ronnie his Miranda rights, Roche said, Please sign if you want to talk." The stress finally broke him.

"My daughter," Ronnie sobbed. "If they find out."

"We'll protect her," Toby said, voice softening. "But we need everything. Now."

Ronnie opened the floodgates. He detailed the whole operation, found players in Colombia, mapped the smuggling routes, even described how they picked couriers, young, desperate, often undocumented.

Here is how it worked. They used airline employees in Colombia and the United States, a system of couriers and lookouts were recruited and developed. A minimum of fifteen flights per week arrived at Miami Airport, with two lookouts in first class, and five couriers, each with less than 50 lbs. in carry-on suitcases. This was to keep under the airlines fifty pounds per carry-on bag limit.

The purpose was to substitute narcotics lost on the streets, and those seized by law enforcement. A trusted narcotics smuggling foreign national who lost significant amounts of cocaine could end up dead very quickly. The purpose and design of the backfilling of the lost narcotics was created and developed by Romero Paez and associates.

When this situation occurred, the criminal enterprise would fill the needs of the cartel. The price of cocaine has always been parallel to the price of gold. For example, if a kilo of gold is valued at $40K per kilo, gold is $40k per kilo. When cocaine was lost during the encounters in Miami, 70% dealer taxation occurred to replace it to avoid repercussions. So, to replace ten kilos would now cost $680,000.00 based on the emergency.

Agent Roche, after specifically speaking with Ronnie, learned that he was to meet a United Airlines employee, by noticing if he would have a handkerchief in his hand, at the entrance to the magnetometer, which was found at the security area at the international concourse. If the passenger saw the airline employee waving the handkerchief, then he/she would wave a similar one back. Then the airline employee would enter security with his airport badge and head to a service elevator on the domestic level.

The airline employee would use his key to send the elevator up to the international Concourse level. Then the two flight lookouts and drug-carrying mules would enter the elevator on an international level and exit the domestic concourse with no interaction with immigration or customs personnel.

Then they would exit the Miami International Airport into a waiting vehicle, with an unchecked 250 lbs. of cocaine to a hotel in the Kendall, Florida area. The product would then be delivered on the streets of the USA.

At the beginning of an active 3-year investigation, Tobias, and Special Agent Mark Kelling of the DEA, along with the Customs Inspectors Jay McNamara and Mike Burns found the airline employee who became the chief informant in Operation Evasion.

Ronnie said, "They pay me through deposits. Lesser amounts. Nothing over ten grand," Ronnie said, pointing to the slips.

"Classic structuring," Mark said to Toby.

Special Agent Neal Rau was dispatched to search Ronnie's car, parked in the employee garage. Inside, they found Magnum condoms tucked beneath the driver's seat and a series of deposit slips, evidence of financial structuring.

Ronnie revealed a deeply personal truth; he was gay and heavily involved in the drug smuggling operation.

"Nobody knows. Not my boss. Not even my daughter. They'd kill me."

For the next six hours, the agents sat with Ronnie as he spilled everything. Toby could feel the gravity of it wasn't just another bust. This was a network unraveling from the inside. After wrapping the interview, they escorted Ronnie to the U.S. Magistrate's Court for his first appearance. He was granted a light bond in exchange for cooperation. But back at his residence, the air turned cold.

"She was here an hour ago," Ronnie said, eyes darting frantically. "My daughter should be home. She never just disappears."

Then came the knock. A sharply dressed man in a tailored suit.

"Who the hell are you?" Ronnie asked.

"I'm an attorney. I stand for the interests concerning Mr. Rodriguez. I suggest we speak as soon as possible.

And so, Operation Evasion, the opening chapter in what would become the next thirty years of Tobias Roche's life.

Chapter IV

The morning of Ronnie's first appearance on the drug and conspiracy charges, Tobias walked into the U.S. Attorney's Office in Miami and began typing the affidavit and criminal complaint. The head of the Narcotics section, Guy Lewis (a future US Attorney for the Southern District of Florida) walked over with a meticulously dressed female.

Lewis said, "Tobias, this is a brand-new Assistant U.S. Attorney, Jackie Arango, and Jackie, this is a "seasoned customs agent" Toby Roche.

To which Roche replied, "Yes, seasoned and overcooked."

It was Jackie Arango's first day of work and her very first case. (She would later in her career become the Chief AUSA of the Government Corruption Division in Miami.) Also, coming over was Paul Pelletier, who was the Senior AUSA within the Narcotics Division (who later became a top U.S. Department of Justice prosecutor in Washington D.C.) More importantly he was a FOT (Friend of Toby) and later became a key part in this case, almost 30 years later!

They didn't know it yet, but what started as a routine bond hearing was about to peel back the curtain on a narcotics operation wrapped in corruption and dirty money. It wasn't just about moving dope; it was about who was protecting it on the inside. Politicians, lawyers, and cowards with their hands out!

Together, Roche, Pelletier, Arango, and Kelling collaborated to get the cooperator (Ronnie) on bond. Roche, Kelling, and the Customs/DEA special agents of FJTG Group 15 had spent the night with Allie at the Wellesley Inn Hotel in Kendall (a western section of Miami), waiting for someone to pick up the fifty pounds of cocaine, for a controlled delivery to its destination. That never occurred.

As the investigation went well into the evening, the agents became hungry and decided to pitch in money for pizza. Money was collected; the only place open was Pizzeria Uno (a Chicago deep dish) that was extremely expensive. A large pizza was ordered and picked up and Big Jose decided to eat half of it himself and screwed his fellow agents. All were pissed off. Even Agent "No Cheese," who never had money but for an allowance he received from his wife complained.

A detail like that sticks with you. You're hunting cartel affiliates in the dead of night, wired tight, low on sleep and caffeine, and a guy hogs the last slice like it's a survival exercise. It wasn't just pizza, it was principle. Brotherhood only works when everyone eats. When Ronnie arrived at his residence, he was shocked to see that his 10-year-old daughter was not home.

Suddenly, the phone rang, and it was an attorney who said he was hired to represent him and would be there in 30 minutes. It was impossible for Ronnie to have reached out to get a lawyer because he had waived his

Miranda Rights and was in Agent Roche's custody for the last twenty-four hours.

The only conclusion was that the Cali Cartel had read the new arrests on the court docket and paid a corrupt Miami lawyer to make an appearance on his behalf, but he had already appeared. Tobias was right in his assessment. Roche and Kelling immediately called Pelletier and Arango and notified them of the situation at hand.

Pelletier, a person of logical and quick decision-making said, "Wire him up."

That was done to do a consensual monitoring, by placing a Niagara recording device concealed under Ronnie's shirt. As the agents hid in the back room of Ronnie's townhouse, the doorbell rang.

Sure enough, it was Don Ferguson, a former AUSA, who came to the door. He stated, "Are you [Ronnie's full name]?"

Ronnie replied, "Yes, sir."

Ferguson then stated, "I am here to represent you," to which Ronnie asked, "How did you know to come here?"

Ferguson, obviously spooked, then said that he must have the wrong person and exited the residence to his vehicle. The Operation Cornerstone task force was notified by Roche and had the Florida Highway Patrol pull over Ferguson's Mercedes and question him. Now Agent Roche and his team knew they were onto something big. What Ferguson didn't know was that he had just stepped on a live wire.

You could see it in his eyes when they lit him up roadside, he wasn't acting like a lawyer anymore. He was sweating like a smuggler at customs. Shaking hands. Fumbling for explanations. And behind those tinted windows. Case files, burner phones, even a throwaway GPS with routes highlighted in red. This wasn't a representation. This was an infiltration.

While waiting for the return of Ronnie's daughter and before the arrival of the local police to report a potential missing person, the agents continued to debrief Ronnie. Ronnie stated that the organization was headed by Carlos Romero Paez, a narco-trafficker out of Barranquilla, Colombia. He stated that Carlos was a badass and was assisted by his wife, Evelyn Bozon Papa in his smuggling endeavors into the Miami Airport. He said the two of them had recruited him and other airline employees at the Miami International Airport to bring in over multi-thousands of kilos of cocaine into Miami over the last 5 years. The flights occurred 3-5 times per week.

The subject admitted being involved and implicated others in the airline industry and from Colombia. The source was let out on bond and created a roadmap of success to the outcome of this case. Agent Roche and Kelling realized they had hit the jackpot with a passenger drug smuggling operation.

The international naro case strategized and involved the National Drug Intelligence Center (NDIC) to have intelligence research specialists, and financial analysts from the

Financial Crimes Enforcement Network (FINCEN) to supplement their investigation. The investigations would involve sixteen people who were the main players. Conspirators from Barranquilla, and Bogota Colombia were the foreign participants. Airline employees from Colombia were the others, including U.S, Citizens.

It soon became clear that Carlo had a family-based business venture. And that was just the first layer. What Ronnie described next would rip through the whole airport like a virus. There were several airport personnel who participated in the smuggling operation. Baggage handlers slid cocaine bricks under the radar.

Even a security screener who ran interference for the couriers. You start pulling on threads like that, soon you're not dealing with couriers, and you're dealing with institutions.

Tobias and his team weren't just chasing dealers. They were chasing systems. Corruption in a tailored suit. Narco money wrapped in attorney-client privilege. That's what Ferguson and others represented: an open door between the courtroom and the cocaine trade.

Nobody hires a lawyer like that in thirty minutes. Not unless the call was made for him by someone who didn't want Ronnie talking. The moment Ferguson walked out that door, Tobias knew someone high up was worried.

Not about Ronnie's freedom, but about what he knew. Back at the townhouse, Ronnie sat slumped on the couch.

He looked like a man who had just realized he was a pawn in someone else's game, and the board had flipped. His eyes darted to the window every few seconds. Sweat soaked through his shirt, even with the AC on. He wasn't worried about prison. He was worried about a bullet to the head and his daughter's safety.

"You're not safe here," Roche told him flatly. "Cartel already moved on you once. You think that's the last time?"

Ronnie swallowed hard. "They took my daughter to shut me up."

Nobody said anything for a long moment. That kind of silence cuts deeper than shouting.

Pelletier got on the phone. "We're making this guy a CI right now," he told Roche "He's already in play whether he likes it or not."

The paperwork was done in under ten minutes. Fastest they had ever moved. The agents didn't have time to do the babysit policy. This wasn't some drug courier snitching for points. Ronnie had walked the runway with wolves. He had the flight schedules. The bag numbers. The crew codes. He had names.

Ronnie explained, "Carlos Romero Paez and Evelyn Bozon Papa," he repeated. "She ran it tighter than him. He did the deals, but she made sure they landed."

Roche leaned in. "How did it get through the Barranquilla Airport. Ronnie gave a nervous laugh. "There's no in-country security if your family clears security. That's how. We moved it through like a line production item.

That hit like a gut punch. It meant this wasn't just a leak. This was a pipeline, fueled by family, bribery, and fear. Agent Roche called in back-up and moved Ronnie to a secure hotel.

A real one this time, not some cheap roadside inn. He got a new burner, an alias, and two agents outside his door around the clock. Meanwhile, FJTG Group 15 started pulling airport personnel files. Looking for overlap, marriages, cousins, and bank deposits that didn't add up and might contradict him.

Roche stayed behind. Not to guard Ronnie, but to work him. He knew this kind of cooperator needed pressure and presence. Too much time alone and they would talk themselves out of everything. Especially when they think death's knocking on their door with a silencer.

"We will get your daughter back?" Roche said. "Then talk. Fast. Clean. And full."

Ronnie broke. For the next six hours, Ronnie spoke nonstop. He named the handlers; he mapped out the drops. He told Tobias how they used coffee and Christmas wrap concealed in first-class baggage to avoid scanners and canine checks. Performance base corruption.

"They trained the airline employees," he said. "Like actors. Like robots. Smile. Nod. Wave the right ones through."

Tobias and his team weren't just dealing with traffickers. They were dealing with a well-oiled machine of smugglers.

Chapter V

Ronnie continued to outline the Romero Paez organization. Besides Evelyn Bozon Papa, there was Rafael Mazzelli, who was a supervisor with American Airlines at the Miami International Airport. Mazzelli was a cocky little bastard who was an American citizen of Colombian descent. Also involved was a person named Ivan Dario Estrada, who was a money pickup man from Bogotá, Colombia.

The go-to person for the money operation in the United States was Barbara Romero, another relative. Overseas was a person named Alex Sierra, who coordinated the pickup of the drugs at the Colombian airports in Barranquilla and Bogotá.

A network of trustworthy couriers was organized by Romero-Paez and Bozon Papa to facilitate the prompt delivery of narcotics to the principals who had lost or had seized kilos of cocaine, so that the families in Colombia would not be murdered.

This wasn't some street-corner crack crew. This was a multilevel logistics machine with the precision of FedEx and the paranoia of a cartel death squad. It ran on silence, blood loyalty, and the fear of waking up in a ditch if you fumbled a kilo.

AUSAs Arango and Pelletier convened a federal grand jury to get subpoenas out for testimony of agents, principals, and documentary evidence. Agents Roche and Kelling obtained the shipping documents for the suitcases used in the cocaine smuggling operation and was not astonished to learn that they had been purchased at Costco in Kendall, Florida, and shipped to Colombia for packing with Christmas wrapping and coffee to deter the U.S. Customs canines.

At Costco, both agents began to laugh when looking at the luggage. The name of the luggage was "The Smuggler." The Romero Paez organization did not speak English, and this was the cheapest luggage that was sold and sent in bulk to Colombia.

"Jesus," Kelling said. "They named the damn bag The Smuggler. This whole case writes itself."

Agents No Cheese and Tater were busy getting the free food samples by flirting with the Latin ladies who were serving them on small plates. Yes, there is a free lunch. Especially when you flash a cocky grin and a stupid smile!

Agents Roche and Kelling also worked closely with the U.S. Customs Passenger Analysis Unit (PAU) and the Rover Customs Inspectors at Miami International Airport. The professionalism of everyone resulted in the development of great conspiracy cases. It wasn't simply good police work; it was tight, seamless coordination between departments that usually hated each other's guts.

In this rare instance, the mission came first. Egos took a back seat. No pissing contests, just results. Locally, the FJTG was able to obtain all the seizures involving "The Smuggler" Luggage.

Including the defendants' arrested and abandoned contraband in the airport concourses and restrooms.

Kelling, also known as Agent Cute by the U.S. Attorney's Office, suggested that they contact the newly formed National Drug and Intelligence Center in Johnstown, Pennsylvania. Help was needed with telephone analysis, pen registers, timing between phone calls from the cell phone records of the Miami co-conspirators to Colombian drug movement contacts, to secure the lookouts and couriers on the airplane flights.

The feds from Johnstown were cold-weather desk warriors, soft hands, no tans, but sharp as scalpels.

They didn't chase dope boys down alleys, but they could crack encrypted call logs like old bones.

Agent Roche spoke with NDIC Director Michael Horn of the DEA. A bond was formed, and they agreed to send six intelligence research specialists from the cold of Pennsylvania to the warmth of Florida for several months to work on the dry conspiracy of the investigation.

They came down like lab rats in button-downs, stared at the whiteboards, drank vending machine coffee, and decoded webs of burner phones with the enthusiasm of surgeons in an autopsy room. Nobody cared about overtime. This was an all-out Narco War. Agent Roche would always find humor in that Agent Cute would go with him to various bars and clubs in Kendall and would attract a cult following of Latin Female patrons at Café Iguana and Keg South. Tobias was a devoted husband, but enjoyed watching Mark get drinks sent to the table.

Waiters would tell him (Kelling) that he had a secret admirer, and he would respond that he couldn't accept the free offer. Roche would grab the drink and respond as he chugged it, "I have a wife, and there is no obligation, and what makes you think it was a woman, Mark?"

That line became a classic inside joke at Group 15. The agents in Group 15 would go to El Torrito's at International Mall every Thursday night and feast on $1 margaritas, $1 draft beers, and a free Mexican buffet.

For $10 you could be feeling no pain and reliving stress from the week's work on controlled deliveries, arrests, and seizures.

That bar was their confession booth, church pew, and war room. They toasted to seizures, roasted each other mercilessly, and planned their next moves over stale nachos and bottom-shelf tequila. The FJTG gave Toby some lifetime loyal friends. Sam Weitz, who was a powerlifter and worked part-time for WCW wrestling; recently transferred Paul DeCotis, who was recently married to a friend and former colleague, and Robert Murphy, who was the first to help with a case.

These were the best of the best, agents who didn't chase headlines, just results. And they had open contempt for butt-snorkelers, ribbon chasers, and paper-shuffling ride-along agents who showed up clean and left clueless. The group also had characters such as Jose and Tater, who almost drove off with a kilo of cocaine on top of his government car, and who entered the wrong bay at an industrial area, putting the wrong people on the ground.

It was also great to work with DEA Supervisor Jimmy "Cool Breeze" Williams, who was respected by members of Group 15. Some of the pranks included dumping fart bomb fireworks in new G-Rides and putting Vaseline in agents' shoes while they went out running or were at the gym. "You didn't just earn your place, you survived it."

It was decided by Pelletier that Tobias should interview Rafael Mazzelli at the Miami International Airport and see if he wanted to cooperate. Mazzelli listened to what the agents had to say, but at the interview, stated, "When you have something, arrest me. Until then, go fuck yourselves."

He then left. Roche called the duty AUSA, who said this could wait until tomorrow, but tomorrow never came, and Mazzelli disappeared from the United States. Such coins the phrase: "If you snooze, you lose."

As previously discussed, Ronnie's daughter was missing from his residence. A day later, Evelyn Bozon Papa returned with the daughter and other family members. Roche, Kelling, No Cheese, Agent Neal Rau, and Murphy immediately went to Ronnie's residence.

Upon arrival, the female members of Evelyn's family, sitting on the stairs, stared at Agent Cute, looked like he was a member of Menudo, a Hispanic boy band. Roche encountered Evelyn and asked where she was. Evelyn told Tobias that everyone went on a mini vacation to Orlando. Roche told her that was bullshit. He implied that she was hiding Carlos (husband) and was well aware of what was going on.

Evelyn then cursed Tobias in Spanish. Ronnie then intervened and told Evelyn, "Listen, cousin, these people are trying to help you, and things will only get worse if you don't talk with them."

Evelyn then replied in Spanish, "Fuck this son of a bitch (Roche). I am not going to talk with him and suggest you do the same."

She then got into a prepaid taxi with her children and was taken away. So, the pursuit continued..

Chapter VI

Where is Carlos? Carlos Romero Paez had disappeared from the grid. Roche and Kelling decided to take Ronnie down memory lane. They loaded him into an unmarked Chevy Camaro, drove south through Miami traffic like sharks chasing blood, and pulled into the Kendall area. This was prime narco-territory back then. Suburban streets, cookie-cutter houses with million-dollar secrets buried behind stucco and palm trees.

According to Ronnie, this was where Carlos kept his stash houses, tucked neatly between dentists' offices and strip mall gyms. Cocaine and cash living side-by-side with soccer moms and retirees. They told Ronnie to wait in the car, cracked the windows, and left the engine running. Kelling slipped a Glock under his jacket. Roche racked a round quietly into his Glock19 also. Old habits die hard! You never knew when a dope house visit could turn into a gunfight.

The address provided was a tan single-story with fake orange Spanish tiles on the roof. A spot pointed out earlier by a cultivated source, one they trusted just enough to bet their lives on. Inside they could see food still on the table. A box from Islas Canarias, greasy and still warm. Cuban sandwiches, croquetas, and black beans. Receipts timestamped just thirty minutes earlier.

The door was unlocked. Guns up. Fast entry. No yelling, no wasted movement. Only an empty house, but the smell of cigarette smoke still hung in the air like a ghost. Carlos had been there. And he'd bolted. Agent Roche found a duffel bag ripped open on the floor, bundles of rubber bands but no cash. Kelling checked the bathroom, saw wet towels. Someone had taken a quick shower, grabbed a go-bag, and ran.

Carlos had obviously been spooked. Word was, his corrupt Colombian lawyers had arrived with fictitious documents, bogus Venezuelan passports, and a well-rehearsed exit plan. Carlos had the cash. He had the paperwork. Now all he needed was a plane ticket and a thirty-minute head start.

Thus, the name "Operation Evasion" was created. It wasn't just catchy. It was survival.

Based on the seizure of the $500,000 from Barbara Romero's vehicle, it was learned that the courier was Ivan Dario Estrada.

A Colombian kingpin with a taste for drama and a sick sense of humor. Estrada wasn't your typical cartel heavy.

He was a cross-dresser. A heavyset figure with a five o'clock shadow, bad lipstick, and worse fashion sense. He'd hit South Beach clubs dressed like he was auditioning for a "Ladies' Night" commercial from the nineteen-eighties, a linebacker squeezed into a sequined mini dress. Hysterical and horrifying all at once.

Group 15 agents periodically tailed Estrada, logging his movements, building the case piece by piece. But Estrada was no fool. He knew the heat was on. He slipped out of Miami using a forged ID that would've fooled even the best Customs inspectors.

Gone. Back to Bogota. Strike one for the bad guys. Now it was time to focus on Evelyn.

The AUSAs decided it was time to subpoena her to the grand jury for Operation Evasion. The evidence had been gathered. The witnesses debriefed. The case analysis was accomplished, running parallel with the work done by the National Drug Intelligence Center. It was airtight. Roche and Kelling personally served Evelyn Bozon-Papa with the grand jury subpoena. They caught her outside her lawyer's office, stepping out of a gleaming black BMW like she didn't have a care in the world.

She stared them down, coldly. Bozon Papa said, "The Special Agents could take a quick trip to hell."

Typical cartel arrogance. Several days later, Evelyn, flanked by her slick Miami attorney, marched into the federal courthouse to testify. Everyone figured she would do what cartel narco traffickers always did: hide behind the Fifth Amendment, like it was a bulletproof vest. But before she even got a chance to open her mouth, AUSA Paul Pelletier intercepted her in the hallway outside the grand jury room. Pelletier didn't smile. He wasn't there to play games.

"Ms. Bozon Papa," Pelletier said, in a firm voice and no bullshit. "The government appreciates you coming under subpoena today to appear before the grand jury. Unfortunately, in the last 15 minutes, you've been indicted for federal drug smuggling charges with conspiracy provisions."

Evelyn blinked. Didn't move. Like someone had cut the strings off a puppet. Tobias Roche stepped forward, cuffs in hand. Read her the warrant. Snapped the bracelets on her wrists with a clean, professional click. Showtime.

Evelyn was processed at the U.S. Marshals Office and transported to the women's detention center. Based upon the seriousness of the offense and her obvious flight risk, the judge denied bond. No ankle bracelets. No bailouts. She was stuck.

She refused to cooperate, clinging to the cartel fantasy that her lawyers could pull a rabbit out of a hat. Nothing could be further from the truth. Her main defense attorney, Neil Nameroff, floated the idea of using the "battered wife defense," which was a Hail Mary pass into the teeth of a federal system that had no patience for sob stories. Federal prosecutors Pelletier and Arangom, with Roche and Kelling standing by, crushed that idea in one meeting.

"This isn't family court," Pelletier said bluntly. "This is a narcotics conspiracy. She's going down."

Nameroff, greasy even by Miami defense attorney standards, wasn't done scheming. He was known to haunt Tobacco Road, a downtown bar where feds and AUSAs grabbed beers after work. Nameroff would sit at the corner of the bar, nursing whiskey, eavesdropping, and taking mental notes on who got drunk and who talked loose. A bottom-feeder if there ever was one. The trial of Evelyn Bozon-Papa was set.

Witnesses lined up. Evidence cataloged and boxed, motion hearings argued and ruled on. It was now game time.

The Honorable Joan Lenard, newly elevated to the federal bench from Florida family court, presided. She wasn't flashy, but she was smart, fair, and moved proceedings like a surgeon with a scalpel. No drama. No nonsense. Evelyn's trial was a disaster for Evelyn.

The battered wife defense got thrown out with the trash. The circumstantial evidence against her was overwhelming. Dozens of documents. Wire transfers. Bank records. Witness testimony. Surveillance photos.

Even recordings of Evelyn herself, cold as ice, talking about "losing shipments" and "making the customers whole." The jury didn't need long. Convicted. Slam dunk.

Several days later, Evelyn Bozon-Papa became a piece of federal judicial history. She became the first federal female criminal defendant to receive a double life sentence without parole for drug smuggling. Federal Judge Joan Lenard hammered her with the maximum/mandatory under the sentencing guidelines set during President George H.W. Bush's "War on Drugs" era.

When Lenard read the sentence aloud, Evelyn crumpled like wet paper. Dropped to her knees in open court, sobbing hysterically as U.S. Marshals dragged her away. She got more time than the infamous Griselda

Blanco, the Black Widow/La Madrina of Medellin. Afterward, Roche, Pelletier, Kelling, and Arango rode the courthouse elevator down in stunned silence. It wasn't joy. It wasn't gloating.

It was the stunning realization that justice, true justice, had just punched through the cartel armor. In the elevator, Pelletier looked around and said, "This is just the beginning. "There were others: Carlos, Ivan, Rafael, and half a dozen more ghosts hiding in the sun-drenched sprawl of Miami and Colombia.

Everyone nodded grimly. No speeches. No high-fives. Just work to do.

Several days later, Evelyn was shackled up and placed on a prison transport bus bound for FCI Tallahassee, a women's maximum-security federal prison. Double life. No parole. No deals. Operation Evasion had gutted the organization. The largest passenger narcotics smuggling ring in Miami International Airport history had been smashed to pieces. There would always be more dope. More players. More money. But for now? *For a brief moment, the good guys one. Bad guys zero. And that was good enough.*

Senior Agent Roche's U.S. Government shield

The brains of the narcotic operation, Carlos Romero Paez and Evelyn Bozon Papa

The Smuggler luggage used by Evelyn and Carlos's in the Miami Airport drug smuggling operation

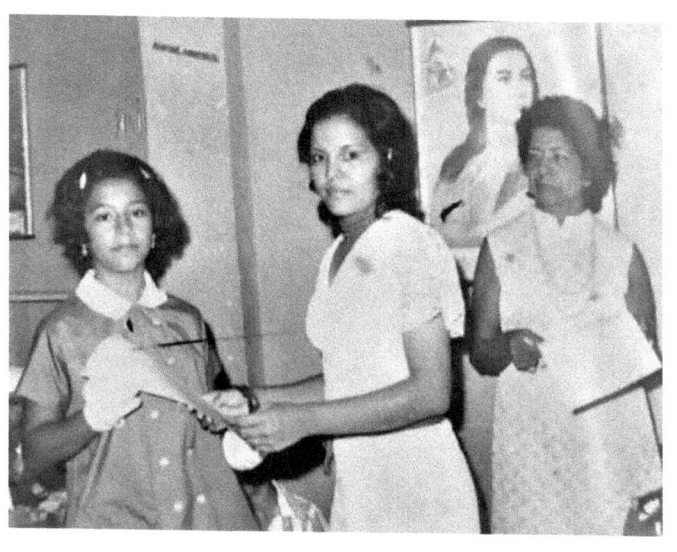

Evelyn with her family as a teenager

A young Evelyn at her Quince (15 years old)

Evelyn in Miami

Tobias when he was a Florida boxing commissioner

Paul Pelletier and Tobias Roche

Tobias and Evelyn at MacDonalds the day of her release

Evelyn, Tobias, and Martha in Bogota, Columbia

Chapter VII

Focus was now on the other principals of the investigation. As mentioned before, Tobias had an adversarial relationship with the senior managers of the U.S. Customs Office in Miami. This wasn't the friendly kind of rivalry you joke about at the bar after work. It was blood deep.

There was one of them, a smiling backstabber, who orchestrated agent Roche's transfer off "Operation Dutybound," the most successful undercover fraud venture U.S. Customs has ever touched. Dutybound had bled into the gold money laundering mess of Polar Cap IV, a case that ripped open the textile-based illegal market. Agent Roche had created it. Built it from scratch. Made it work. And they still yanked him.

The coward who pulled it off had started his career not in law enforcement, but slinging whiskey as a bartender in some seedy NYC joint, serving drinks to Customs agents who were doing real work while he kissed ass for tips.

The other high-level "leader," also a proud son of New York, had a reputation for handing out promotions based on your batting average, not your arrest record. If you could hit a double in the agency softball game, you got a gold star. If you arrested twenty smugglers? You got detailed to an obscure border location. That kind of culture turned the SAC/Miami into a snake pit. Good agents were stabbed in the back, while lazy ones were promoted because they could swing a softball bat. Tobias didn't miss it.

Now at the Florida Joint Task Group (FJTG), Toby finally worked among professionals, real agents who gave a damn about the job and had each other's backs. Tobias had a source of information whom he called "Deep Throat." Old school. Anonymous. Untouchable. Deep Throat was dying. Lung cancer had torn him up from the inside out.

Tobias got the call urgently. He drove like a maniac through Miami traffic to Kendall Regional West Hospital. Tobias found the old man gasping under an oxygen tent, skin the color of week-old newspaper. He motioned Tobias closer. Voice like sandpaper, "Maselli's teenage son was going to visit him in Dallas." Tomorrow for sure. That's all he had the strength to say. That's all Toby needed to hear.

Roche squeezed his hand, a rare show of respect, and left the hospital. There was no time for sentiment.

Back at the Customs SAC field office, Roche packed a suitcase, updated his weapon and travel paperwork, and went upstairs to notify the fugitive coordinator and the Special Agent in Charge. Time was everything. Mazelli had disappeared off the grid over seven years ago, running like a rabbit once he caught word of his indictment. Hiding out somewhere overseas, bouncing between safehouses and fake names.

This was the one shot. Follow the son to the airport. Get on the same flight to Dallas. Snag Mazelli at the gate where he would least expect it.

Unarmed. Exposed. Clean takedown. But no. The fugitive coordinator shook his head. The Special Agent in Charge, a legend in his own mind, who wasn't sure if he was Hispanic or Italian known as "SAC Sleaze"{thanks, to a scandal involving "missing" funds when he ran the San Juan office}, had denied the travel request.

No reason given. No logic offered. Tobias laughed profusely "Fuck him and his small brain mentality. "Screw protocol. Toby called his friends in the U.S. Marshals Service. Real operators who got the job done without asking for the softball stats first. Toby fully explained the situation in detail to them and what occurred. Tomorrow, a flight to Dallas, and the U.S. Marshals didn't hesitate.

They threw together a surveillance team overnight. Camped outside Mazelli's son's residence. Drank bad coffee. Took shifts. Sure enough, in the early morning, the kid came out. He got into a taxi. The U.S. Marshals tailed him to Miami International Airport. Watched him go through security. Boarded the same plane. The call went out to Dallas: "Be ready. "Touchdown in Dallas.

The Miami U.S. Marshals stayed glued to the kid, following close but not too close. Professional. Unseen. And there he was, Rafael Mazelli. The subject was waiting at the gate. Smug and cocky as ever. A new eighteen-year-old Colombian wife was clinging to his arm. A newborn baby in a carrier. Playing the family, person. Masking the rot underneath.

One of the Dallas deputies, wearing a U.S. Marshals belt buckle badge, leaned casually against a wall. Mazelli's eyes locked on that badge. Fight or flight kicked in. Mazelli chose flight. He dumped the infant onto a chair like a sack of groceries and bolted.

Agents swarmed. Through the concourse. Past screaming civilians. Security alarms blaring. Mazelli ran like a terrified ten-year-old boy, arms flailing, no plan, just pure animal panic.

Deputies tackled him just before he hit the main security checkpoint. Slammed him face-first onto the linoleum. Cuffed him tight. No Miranda warnings. No negotiation. Just done.

They transported him to his Dallas residence under his phony driver's license. Search warrant in hand. U.S. Marshals deputies found inside the residence, fake passports. Colombia, Spain, England, and Italy. Mazelli had been bouncing around Europe, hiding like a cockroach under hotel beds. He waived extradition, a smart move, and was flown back to Miami to face the music.

In Miami federal court, they dragged him out in a bright orange U.S. Bureau of Prison jumpsuit. No more Rolexes and Gucci shoes. No more designer suits. No more smirks. They seated him in the jury box for arraignment. Shackled. First row, courtroom left: Roche, Kelling, Arango, and Pelletier.

Agent Roche leaned forward. Grinned and said, "I guess we got fucking something on you now."

Mazelli said nothing. Just stared at the floor. He was cooked. 15 years for his role in Operation Evasion. Ronnie was there too. Watched the whole thing. Didn't say a word. Just burned a hole through Mazelli with his stare. Ronnie would do five years, bought, and paid for with his cooperation.

The remaining fugitives? Alex Serra. Organizer of transportation in Colombia. Ivan Dario Estrada. The cross-dressing heavy hitter. And the boss. Carlos Romero Paez. Romero Paez was back in Colombia and Panama, living like a prince. Running a "Compra Venta" money laundering operation under the cover of jewelry stores. Moving cash like freight. Still tied to the Cali Cartel. Still pulling strings while his wife rotted in a Florida maximum security federal prison.

Tobias wasn't done. Through sources, he got Carlos's burner phone numbers. Took a Spanish translator with him. Started making calls. Tobias desperately tried to bring Carlos in. Agent Roche promised him a deal if he surrendered.

Tobias said, "Help your wife, help yourself."

Carlos played along, and he also made promises. Carlos even agreed to a plane pickup, a C-130 flight from Panama to the U.S. Toby set the whole thing up. Carlos ghosted him. The scumbag never showed.

That was no surprise to Agent Roche. He knew that Carlos was a no-good lowlife narco, great to his children, but with no conscience. On the run, Carlos lived like a king one day and an alley rat the next. He was stabbed twice. Probably by his own "friends."

Then, everything for years went silent. Six months after Tobias retired as a Supervisory Special Agent in 2006, a call came in from Mark Kelling. Mark said this urgently. "Carlos is dead." DEA in Bogota confirmed it. Kelling sent the newspaper article and the crime scene photos. Carlos Romero Paez. Gunned down in Barranquilla. Driving a brand-new BMW. Two motorcycle assassins pulled up alongside him. Masked. Armed. Sprayed the car with automatic rifle fire. Left him and his passenger shredded inside.

The pictures were quite graphic, to say the least; they were horrific. Chunks of flesh blown apart, body parts. Blood splattered across shattered glass. A scene straight out of a cartel execution manual. No courtroom justice. No prison time. Just the cold calculus of the drug world. Live by the sword. Die by the sword. The outcome was not justice. It was just revenge. Among thieves. Among killers.

Chapter VIII

Any good federal agent periodically checks the U.S. Bureau of Prisons Inmate Locator website to see the status of persons that they have arrested (past and present).

They also check the U.S. Department of Homeland Security website for deportations. This is done for personal safety of the agent. If you were a "pencil pusher" or "ride along" then you don't have to do this because you're a leech to your agency, without the mental capacity to do investigations. Such was the case which caused a life-changing event for Tobias Roche.

In early 2021, Roche was checking the status of both systems concerning inmates. He was curious to see if Evelyn Bozon Papa was still serving her two life sentences in Maximum Security Federal Prison for Women in Tallahassee, Florida. She was indeed serving her life sentences. While checking the computer, Tobias accidentally hit a mouse click which brought him to the internet page on Evelyn to include advocacy for her release.

Tobias said to himself, "This must be a bunch of bullshit, recalling how she was in the middle 1990's".

Roche noticed a video put out by The Cando Foundation, created by former federal inmate and prison release advocate Amy Povah Ralston. The YouTube video was conducted by Evelyn's daughter, Martha Romero, whom Roche remembered when she was a 10-year-old girl sitting on the stairs when the FJTG agents first encountered her mother. The mid to late thirties woman in the video was pleading for someone to help her mother come home.

Tobias watched the video intensely and, in the conclusion, this hard-nosed and conservative person had nearly been brought to tears! If everything was true as stated, then Roche decided right then and there to look into the current life of Evelyn, almost 30 years later. The video spoke about how Bozon Papa was a model federal prisoner.

When Roche first spoke with former AUSA Pelletier and DEA agent Kelling, they both said, "You're calling me about Evelyn, right?" It was astonishing to hear the same thing from both. Both immediately supported Tobias looking into the matter. Martha Romero, Liz Mendoza, and Damaris Ramos

Hernandez immediately provided Roche with specific information about correctional officers, counselors, and former inmates who were incarcerated with her.

Both Liz and Damaris had served time with Evelyn in the FBOP Tallahassee and viewed her as a second mother. Thus, the team was launched to begin the quest for the possible release of Evelyn.

The team looked at clemency, pardon, and compassionate release. There is a saying in law enforcement: time doesn't forget. It doesn't heal, either. It just. hardens. Sets like cement. But now and then, time throws a curveball that hits you square in the chest and cracks the concrete wide open. That's what happened to Tobias Roche in 2021.

He was not a desk jockey, punching the clock and waiting for his pension. Roche had made a career in blood, betrayal, and case files stacked higher than most agents ever lived to see. The kind of guy who never slept too easily because the ghosts he had put away sometimes knocked back.

He checked those inmate locators not for fun, not out of morbid curiosity, but because survival taught him to. If someone he put away got out, or worse, disappeared off the radar, it could mean someone was out there, possibly hunting for him. He had seen it happen before. Hit lists were not just cartel mythology, they were real, inked, whispered, and mailed in code.

That day, though, the system didn't just talk back. It screamed.

Bozon Papa, Evelyn. WTF! The quiet queen of silent corridors and thousand-kilo runs. The one woman who stood behind a drug empire with the poise of a politician and the mind of a tactician. Toby remembered the day they took her down like it was tattooed behind his eyes.

Miami heat, half a dozen feds, her daughter on the stairs, wide-eyed and nervous, and Evelyn sitting calm, as if the weight of the world had just caught up to her.

And now this, an advocacy video? Sympathy campaigns? Tobias's gut twisted with old instincts. "No fucking way," he muttered. But curiosity, the kind that kept agents alive, made him click.

And there she was, her daughter. Not the kid from the staircase, but a grown woman with the same quiet eyes and a fire behind them. Martha Romero wasn't begging. She was laying out facts, cold as case files: Evelyn had changed. She wasn't the woman she once was. She was a model inmate. Counselor to the broken. Advocate for those left behind in the belly of the beast. Tobias stared, heart thudding like a slow drum.

He didn't cry. Guys like him don't shed tears for hardened criminals. But something cracked. Something rusted shut for three decades creaked open just enough to let in a question. What if she really wasn't that woman anymore? It wasn't long before he picked up the phone.

Pelletier. Kelling. Brothers in arms from the old days. Federal knights in tailored suits and worn-out shoes. When he brought up Evelyn's name, both of them nailed it before he even finished the sentence. "You're calling me about Evelyn, right?"

That's when it hit him. Maybe this wasn't just a fluke. Maybe the ripple from that click went deeper than he thought. This wasn't just some Hail Mary from a convict's daughter. People were listening. People who once chased Evelyn with handcuffs now paused and said, "Let's talk."

The team came together fast. Like a task force being resurrected from the grave. Martha, Liz, and Damaris. They weren't agents. But they had scars and stories that carried weight. Liz and Damaris walked on the same concrete floors at FCI Tallahassee, that Evelyn had. Ate the same slop. Heard the same 3 a.m. cries in the dark. And they didn't just speak to her; they called her mother. There's a gravity in that word when it comes from a cellblock. Mother. Not just a caretaker. Not just comfort. Protector. Healer. Leader.

So, Roche started digging, not like a prosecutor. Like a man haunted by loose ends. He called old contacts with ICE in Miami and Tallahassee and started vetting claims. They weren't fabrications. They were gospel. Correctional officers said Evelyn de-escalated fights before they turned into bloodbaths.

Counselors said she taught classes that cut recidivism in half. Inmates said she stopped suicides. Evelyn Bozon Papa, the woman he once helped chain to a wall of life sentences, became the career counselor the prison never hired. So, now came the hard part. The paperwork. The petitions. The politics. Tobias helped file for clemency. Dug into compassionate release. Wrote declarations. Leaned on reputations earned in the fire. Pelletier drafted his own letters. Kelling whispered in ears that mattered.

People like Amy Povah opened doors that usually took crowbars and career-ending favors. But this wasn't about redemption. Roche didn't believe that. He believed in truth, raw and bare. And if the truth had changed, if Evelyn had changed, then it was time someone wrote that into the record.

Still, Toby wasn't a fool. He knew some agents would spit at the idea.

"You going soft?" they'd say. "You're supporting the release of a narco trafficker who received two life sentences without the possibility of parole." No. He hadn't. Not for a second.

But he also knew prisons were full of dead women still breathing. And maybe Evelyn had found a way to live.

He didn't owe her. He owed the truth. And the truth? It was evolving.

The real story wasn't just what Evelyn did in the nineties. It was what she did with her time after. Behind concrete walls and razor-tipped fences. In the dark. Without applause or camera crews. A life sentence lived with purpose wasn't exoneration, but it was something.

Tobias Roche hadn't softened. He had sharpened like a Templar Knight's sword. And he was just getting started.

Chapter IX

With the help of her siblings, Martha Romero and Roche attempted to locate the two outstanding individuals who were still wanted from the initial indictment and believed to be in Colombia. Alex Serra, the airport drug fixer, and narcotics transportation organizer from Colombia, knew Martha when she was young. Martha began to research vital records in Barranquilla and matched a family photo. Serra had died of a massive heart attack in the late 1990s.

Also, through a family connection, she learned Ivan Dario Estrada was serving a life sentence for narcotics at the maximum-security prison in Bogota, Colombia. This gave resolution to those who had been indicted in the case and cleared the way for advocacy for

Evelyn's release. Roche conveyed this information to Kelling who notified the DEA/Miami agent in charge of fugitives of the outcome of Martha's research and the validation documents sent to him (Kelling). Roche also began to speak with the advocates on Evelyn's release pertaining to the prison officials, counselors, and religious ministers.

He also established a working relationship with Attorney Carla La Roche (Evelyn's appeal attorney). La Roche was a civil rights and clemency lawyer at the Florida State University Advocacy Center. She and her students worked on inmates' cases from the US Penitentiary for Women in Tallahassee, Florida. To call Roche and La Roche's backgrounds and beliefs about bipolar would be a maximum understatement. Tobias was the ultra-conservative law enforcement officer, while Carla was a liberal and pro-release attorney. Both wondered if this could be a formable team that could achieve their respective goals.

One of the first things they agreed on was to try to get Bozon Pappa clemency from President Donald Trump before he left office on January 20, 2021. There was a problematic assertion that Ronnie's daughter had been kidnapped by Evelyn to attempt to coerce his testimony.

Initially, the local police were contacted to report a missing person, but since Ronnie and Evelyn were related it would not have bearing on Evelyn's request for clemency. Both Toby and Carla agreed that Ronnie should be interviewed about 30 years later. Roche and PI Lazaro Dominguez went to Ronnie's house. Ronnie, now in his eighties, answered the door. He did not immediately recognize Roche. Tobias then reintroduced himself and Ronnie seemed shocked to see him after all these years!

Roche told Ronnie why he was here. He stated he wanted to speak with Ronnie's daughter about the incidents that occurred almost 30 years ago. It concerned Evelyn taking her and other family members on vacation.

Ronnie stated that he did not have any trouble with that and reached out to her at work, as she now held a government job. Roche and Dominguez then left.

Several days later both investigators returned and spoke with Ronnie's daughter. She was now a woman in her thirties but recalled that when she left with Evelyn's family and at no time felt under duress or intimidation. Also, a copy of police reports concerning Ronnie's residence, and there was never a missing person's report on file. Case closed so you would think.

Besides Pelletier and Kelling supporting Evelyn's release, Damaris and Liz interviewed former inmates and staff members to document with Carla and her Florida State University team. It was determined the best course of action was to submit this proffer for release to the U.S. Pardon Attorney for screening to President Trump for clemency or pardon action. A member of the legal committee from California, who was ill informed of Evelyn's entire case, asked Roche to submit an affidavit regarding his interview with Ronnie's daughter regarding his disappearance from the scene shortly after Ronnie's previous arrest.

Tobias immediately complied with the request with a complete and concise explanation. Unfortunately, due to the legal committee members' incompetence, the petition never reached President Donald Trump's desk for consideration. Roche believes to this day that the member withheld this information due to embarrassment from false assertions.

He further stated "that if this clemency and/or pardon reached President Trump's desk for a signature, he surely would have signed it. She was the perfect choice for such action."

President Trump fully supported the First Step Act, spearheaded by former federal Inmates Amy Povah Ralston and Alice Mae Johnson, and Evelyn Bozon Papa was a great candidate to support her release. Tobias was very pissed off by this inaction by an incompetent person. On January 20, 2021, there was no Justice for Evelyn.

The clock was ticking like a goddamn time bomb. January 20th was circled in blood red. Not on a calendar, but in every conversation, Tobias had with Carla La Roche, every whispered phone call with Pelletier, every sleepless night staring at the ceiling thinking about a woman who should have been freed years ago.

They were not allies by nature, Tobias and Carla. Oil and water. Cop and crusader. The hardline fed and the idealist with a law degree and a dream of prison reform. But fate has a sick sense of humor. Somehow, this unlikely pairing turned into a two-pronged battering ram, smashing against the walls of bureaucracy and time.

What united them wasn't Evelyn herself; it was the evidence. It was the truth that nobody could ignore it anymore. Evelyn wasn't just a rehabilitated inmate; she was the institutional spine of the inmates in the prison. Staff leaned on her more than they did their own protocols.

Inmates followed her like she was some kind of light in a place made of shadows and wire.

And now, they had confirmation that the remaining fugitives were no longer threats. Alex Serra was dead; his heart blew out like a tire on a dirt road. Estrada was buried behind bars so deep in Bogotá, he probably forgot what sunlight looked like. With them crossed off the list, there were no more loose ends. No more "what ifs." The table was clean.

Martha Romero was relentless. She dug like a reporter chasing a career-making headline. She burned through Colombian records and shook family trees until something fell out. Her hustle brought answers, cold, hard, and definitive evidence. That meant Evelyn's case was ready for a second look.

So, Tobias picked up the phone again. This time not to an agent or a lawyer, but to the past. It was Ronnie. The last living question mark. The man was old now, wrinkled by decades, probably more used to talking to his TV than real people. When he opened that door and saw Roche standing there, it was like the dead showed up for coffee.

Tobias gave him the rundown. Kept it straight. No spin. Just facts. He did not want to stir the pot, just get the girl's side of the story, the one who was supposedly kidnapped. It was a bullshit rumor, floated back in the day to taint Evelyn's name even more. And sure enough, the daughter, now a grown woman with a government job and a memory as sharp as a razor, told them what really happened.

Vacation. That's all it was. A trip. No guns, no threats, no duffel bags full of silence. Just kids being kids and a woman trying to be an aunt, not a monster. The police officers never filed a report because there was nothing to report. Ronnie didn't protest. Just nodded, maybe relieved that this last ghost was being buried without drama. He wasn't proud of his past, and he didn't fight the truth.

Case closed, again. Or so Toby thought. Then came the legal grease fire. The U.S. Pardon Attorney Committee member. That's where the wheels came off. Instead of pushing the proffer through the right channels, getting it in front of the U.S. Pardon Attorney, routing it to the top, they stalled, fumbled, and maybe even buried it on purpose. But nothing happened.

No movement. No buzz. No follow-up. That's when Toby realized something stunk. That committee member hadn't made a mistake. They'd pulled the pin on the whole damn effort and let it drop. Maybe out of embarrassment. Maybe out of ego. Maybe because admitting Evelyn deserved mercy meant admitting they had been wrong. And nobody in government wants to eat that kind of crow.

So, while thousands of cases passed across desks in D.C., while President Trump put his name on clemencies and pardons, Evelyn's case never even saw daylight. Not even a whisper of consideration.

Tobias knew President Trump's stance. He'd read the speeches. Heard the support for the First Step Act. Seen Amy Povah and Alice

Johnson standing on the White House lawn. Evelyn's case would've been a home run. On paper. On politics. On principle. But the shot never came.

And on January 20, 2021, the door slammed shut with a steel bang. Trump left office. And Evelyn stayed in her cage.

Toby stated, "If Even Bozon Papa's clemency case reached the Oval Office, 45 would have surely signed it".

The rage wasn't just about justice. It was about failure, federal failure. It was about watching a crack in the system widen into a canyon because someone did not want to look dumb. He'd spent his life hunting criminals. Now he was hunting silence. But silence, like cement, doesn't crack easily.

Still, Tobias had not given up. Evelyn was still breathing. Still fighting. And the war wasn't over. Not by a long shot.

Chapter X

Tobias at once phoned Paul Pelletier (now an attorney in private practice) and informed him of the outcome. Pelletier, a terrific attorney and a person of strong character and moral principles said, "Fuck this shit! I will write the judge."

Paul was truly a man of courage and followed up with what he said. Roche also spoke with Attorney La Roche, and she told him that a request for a compassionate release would be filed. Roche, collaborating with his contacts, got ICE to agree that they would at once deport Evelyn back to Colombia if she were released from federal custody.

Then the most memorable act of justice occurred. Federal Judge Joan Lenard would grant Evelyn Bozon Papa time served, if the U.S. Attorney's Office in Miami would not oppose the granting of such motion before the court, that Tobias Roche (now a private investigator and retired ICE Supervisory Special Agent) would be responsible for assuring that Evelyn would get safely back to Colombia, and he (Roche) volunteered to pay for Bozon Papa's travel, lodging, and plane ticket for her venture back to her home country.

AUSA Frank Tamen (who was now the government attorney to oversee any appeals for the release of Evelyn Bozon Papa) was familiar with both Roche and Pelletier, as he had worked cases with both of them.

The second Roche hung up the phone, it was like throwing a lit match into a dry barn. Pelletier exploded. "Let's fucking go Toby, time for her to get her freedom." No hesitation. No fake diplomacy. Just fire. That was Paul. A knife in a suit. A bulldog in a courtroom. He didn't posture. He didn't play defense. He came to win. And when his moral compass locked onto something, God help anyone standing in the way.

Toby had worked with plenty of prosecutors, some slick, some snakes, some too careful for their own good. But Paul Pelletier was the real deal. His loyalty wasn't for sale. His word held weight. Back in the day, they stood shoulder to shoulder taking down drug operations with names longer than their arrest sheets. And now, decades later, that loyalty hadn't wavered an inch.

While Pelletier got busy drafting what would become a personal declaration of war to the court, Tobias kept the wheels turning. He rang up Carla La Roche and gave her the same news. She didn't flinch. "We're filing for compassionate release," she said. Calm, focused, direct. By now, she'd proven she wasn't just another academic with a briefcase full of theory, she was a player. And Tobias, he played his own angle.

He called in favors. Leaned on old contacts from ICE who still picked up the phone when his name flashed on the screen. He didn't have a badge anymore, but his legacy held sway.

They respected the years he gave, the doors he kicked in, the careers he built and sometimes broke. And that respect mattered. ICE agreed, if Evelyn got released, they'd fast-track her deportation back to Colombia. No fuss. No media circus. Quiet exit. Just one woman going home after serving her time. That was the green light. That was the final puzzle piece. Now, it was all in the court's hands. And then came the call. Federal Judge Joan Lenard. Tobias would never forget her name. Ever. The real hero of the criminal justice system.

This wasn't just legal. This wasn't just bureaucratic mechanics grinding along. This was the moment when the justice system, so often blind, slow, or cruel, finally took a breath and looked at the human cost. Judge

Lenard didn't issue lukewarm statements. She didn't couch it in political hedging or bureaucratic hedging. She granted time served. But it came with conditions. Smart ones. Controlled. Thought-out.

The U.S. Attorney's Office in Miami had to agree not to oppose the motion. That was key. Silence from the prosecution was as loud as a marching band in federal court. The second requirement. Tobias Roche himself, now a retired Supervisory Special Agent from ICE, and a full-time private investigator, would personally ensure Evelyn's safe departure. No taxpayer tab. No federal escort. No loopholes. And here's the kicker.

Tobias Roche, the same man who once helped put her in handcuffs and chains, now volunteered to pay for Evelyn's flight home.

Lodging. Plane ticket. Escort. The whole thing. No one told him to. No one asked him to. He just did it. Because at some point in a fed's life, there comes a moment where the badge, the case files, the headlines, they all fade. And what's left is one question: Did you do the right thing? For Roche, this was it.

Meanwhile, down in Miami, a familiar face sat on the government's side of the table: AUSA Frank Tamen. Tamen was no newcomer. He knew how the game worked. A battle-tested federal prosecutor, he would work shoulder to shoulder with Roche and Pelletier on drug cases. He was part of the nineties team. And now, he held sway over any appeals or objections to Evelyn's release. He didn't object.

He respected the weight of this case. The legacy. The players. He knew Evelyn's release wasn't some PR stunt. It was earned, inch by inch, over three decades of tough times, changed lives, and institutional transformation. That silence? That lack of opposition? It was louder than any courtroom outburst.

Because sometimes, not fighting is how justice gets done. Toby looked around at all of it, the paperwork, the court filings, the affidavits, the quiet whispers behind closed doors. And then he remembered the girl from the stairs. Martha Romero. Ten years old back then. Thirty-something now. She'd started the fire. She'd carried her mother's name through years of judgment and stigma. She hadn't stopped moving forward.

Now her mother would walk out of the gate.

It wasn't the kind of story feds usually tell at retirement parties. It wasn't an easy win. There was no SWAT team, no helicopter chase, no final press conference. But it mattered. Because Evelyn Bozon Papa had done her time. And justice, real, unvarnished justice, finally caught up to that fact.

Chapter XI

On April 21, 2021, Tobias Roche went with Liz, Lazaro, and George to the Colombian Consulate in Orlando, Florida. A lot of unusual and unexpected Revelations happened along the way! Evelyn Bozon Papa had been waiting all day in the prison R&D, waiting for the possibility of her release after having received two consecutive life sentences almost 30 years ago, without the possibility of parole.

That day, she said goodbye to the correctional officers and staff, and her adopted daughters (inmates) throughout the long wait that day. Bozon Papa had seen correctional officers get hired and retire while incarcerated. Evelyn had celebrated the release of rehabilitated inmates. Many people were brought to tears. Outside Roche waited for eight long hours for her release by the Bureau of Prisons. All of a sudden, the exterior gate opened, and Evelyn came out in her BOB jumpsuit and quickly climbed into the van, embracing everyone.

Tobias then said to her, "Buenvenida Evelyn de nuevo a los Estados Unidos, Welcome back into the United States."

To which Evelyn laughed and replied, "Toby, of course I know English. I've had 30 years to learn." She then asked Toby, "Have you learned Spanish since I was sent to Tallahassee?" Roche laughed and replied, "I still play the pendejo, the fool!"

Roche then decided that it would be an innovative idea for Evelyn to change to street clothes, because if they were pulled over by a Florida Highway Patrol Trooper (on the way to the Colombia Consulate General's Office in Orlando) it might be a dangerous situation due to the way she was dressed now. The van then pulled into a McDonald's.

As she exited the vehicle with Liz Mendoza, Roche asked Evelyn if she wanted something to eat. Bozon Papa answered that she wanted a Big Mac, large fries, and a Shamrock Shake. Tobias laughed and asked her how she knew about Shamrock Shakes? Evelyn laughed and stated she had seen them on the maximum-security prison TV.

Tobias countered with "It's April Fool's Day, and probably they are discontinued." While Evelyn went in to change, Roche asked the manager if they had any Shamrock Shakes left. The manager came back with the last packet and mixed it for her. While Evelyn ate her first post-incarceration meal, Roche contacted Pelletier and then Kelling on his cell phone. Pelletier was thanked by Evelyn for what he did, and Paul reminded her it was also Good Friday. Evelyn immediately began to sob. When she spoke with Mark Kelling, he told her that he was retiring from the DEA today, and what better way to celebrate with her release. Evelyn continued to cry profusely.

The group then got into the van, and Evelyn continued to chat on Liz's laptop with her family in Colombia. All her children were present on the video chat, and everyone thanked Tobias for everything he did in spearheading and coordinating their mom's release.

Typical Tobias Roche replied, "It was always a team effort, like everything in the criminal justice system." Roche asked Evelyn the question that he waited to ask for almost 30 years.

"How did Carlos Romero Paez escape?"

Evelyn told Roche that when he went to the stash house in Kendall, Carlos barely avoided Roche and Kelling, and that is when he decided to leave the United States. His cartel Colombian lawyers flew to Miami with false documents for him, including bogus passports.

They then assisted Carlos in getting to Nogales, Arizona (a US/Mexico border town). Once there, they rented a helicopter. Romero Paez was a former skilled helicopter pilot for deceased drug kingpin Pablo Escobar. He then flew the rented helicopter under the U.S. Customs radar into Mexico to facilitate his escape. Roche was intrigued with this story.

Tobias then asked about the circumstances of Carlos's assassination and murder. Evelyn stated that he went into business with a female doctor in Barranquilla, to stay in the cocaine exportation enterprise. She decided to eliminate Carlos to maintain total control of the business. The doctor hired two sicarios (hit men) to kill Romero Paez. Shortly after that occurred, she had both of them killed. Dead men tell no tales. Then the Cali Cartel killed the female Colombian doctor turned drug kingpin.

You live by the sword and die by the sword.

Finally, on the drive, Tobias asked Evelyn about her legal pursuit of freedom. Bozon Papa told him that she had a story about Attorney Neal Namaroff of Miami (her trial attorney). Evelyn told Roche that she received a legal call from him in 2009, while she was continuing to serve her consecutive double life sentences.

Namaroff told her that he had Stage 4 cancer and that he was sorry that he had never represented her, just the interest of the Cali Cartel. Tobias told Evelyn that he was a disgrace to the legal profession and that there was a special place in hell for these types of people. *Sold their souls for money.* The legal call was not recorded at the institution, but to this day, Roche believes Bozon Papa's version.

The van arrived in Orlando close to midnight and was met by the Consul General and Attorney La Roche. Once inside the Colombian Consulate, a 30-day temporary passport was issued for Evelyn Bozon Papa and the group then left to get something to eat.

The party of five then went to Denny's to eat. Evelyn had a double Grand Slam along with the others. Real outside non-institution food. Toby picked up the bill and reached out to the hotel. The group arrived at the hotel, and everyone spent the night there. Evelyn had an early morning flight back to Bogota, where she would initially meet her family. The group then arrived at the Orlando International Airport and found the U.S. Customs and Border Protection Officers. Roche had arranged to meet with them the night before, but the CBP Officers inquired where the ICE escort was for the deportee (Bozon Papa).

Tobias replied, "It's me, the retiree." They all laughed. The CBP officers took Evelyn and Roche to the boarding gate and waited for the non-stop flight to board. *It was amazing that she was released to Tobias Roche, a civilian, to take her on the journey home.* This will never happen again. It was truly a miracle, and Toby was given the full trust of others.

All of a sudden, it hit Tobias like a ton of bricks. Evelyn was really going home.

Thirty years ago, they cursed each other in different languages. Now, they were walking toward the gate as human beings.

Everything had come full circle in the criminal justice system. It worked. As Evelyn preboarded the plane, she suddenly turned around and fully embraced Tobias. She told him that she did not know how to thank him.

Roche smiled and replied, "Go back home and be a great mother and grandmother to your children."

Justice Then, and Justice Now.

That night in Orlando, something cracked in Roche that had been calcified for decades. A lifetime of manhunts, wiretaps, seizures, and betrayals. But this was different. This wasn't a bust. It wasn't a takedown. It was a return.

He didn't see a target anymore.

He saw a mother with scars deeper than any case file could capture. A woman who outlasted the concrete and came back to the world changed, not softer, but truer to herself and others. For Tobias, it wasn't absolution. Feds don't do fairy tales. But it was something heavier. Something earned. A full circle reckoning. She was free. And so was he.

EPILOGUE

On April 1, 2022, Tobias Roche knocked on a door located in an apartment complex in Barranquilla, Colombia. A woman replied in Spanish and asked who is it? Roche replied "La Tienda" which means food delivery. The woman then opened the door and immediately started crying and gave him hugs and kisses. It was Evelyn Bozon Papa, who had been released one year to the day from federal prison.

Over the next several days, Toby met all of her family members, including her elderly mom, brothers and sisters, sons and daughters, and grandchildren. It was a joyous occasion, starting with the wonderful co-conspirator for the surprise meeting, her daughter, Martha Romero.

He has remains close to the entire family and is known as Papi and Grandpa Toby. Tobias speaks gleefully about how he was able to reunite Evelyn with her mother after 30 years (who was now in late nineties) and had the opportunity to meet her in Colombia. He now talks regularly with her family in Barranquilla.

He has made several trips and enjoys eating the best cheeseburgers at Puerto's! Tobias is so happy that everything has turned out well for them. All the children are successful human beings, and they have stayed with him in Kendall when they visit the USA. Such is the case with life's twists and unexpected turns.

Given the right situation, people deserve second chances. What Tobias doesn't say outright, but you can see it in his eyes, is that it changed him, too. Seeing Evelyn walk out those gates, a woman who was buried under two life sentences, now hugging her mother after a decade, it shook him. It wasn't just a reunion. It was a resurrection.

Her mother was frail, couldn't walk without a cane, but when she saw her daughter standing in the Colombian sun, free, she stood straighter. No speeches. No tears at first. Just that long, aching silence. That silence you only get when time owes you a debt, and the universe pays it back in full.

Tobias watched the whole thing from a few feet away. Didn't interfere. Just stood there, chewing his gum, sunglasses on, feeling something shift. Shift, deep inside his chest. He thought about his own family, the things he gave up chasing dope runners and dealers, chasing justice, and chasing ghosts. For once, something ended right. He stayed a few weeks in Barranquilla. Met cousins, nieces, nephews. Got invited to a half dozen family dinners. At first, they called him "Señor Tobias," like he was some strange American uncle. By the end of the week, he was just "Toby." They laughed at his Spanish, joked about his gringo tan, and took him out to Puerto's where he got hooked on cheeseburgers slathered with garlic sauce and stacked like skyscrapers.

Tobias found something else down there, too. Not religion, not forgiveness, he was still too tough for that, but something close to peace and tranquility. A kInd of peace that comes with knowing you didn't just destroy, you helped rebuild.

He came back to Miami lighter in thought. Not healed, not fixed, but less haunted. Tobias wishes to thank his close friends who continue to this day to help him in life. Roche is now disabled and struggles day by day with physical disabilities, some attributed to his work in the recovery effort at Ground Zero.

He doesn't like talking about the pain much. The bad joints. The lung issues. The days when just getting out of bed feels like a tactical operation. But if you know him, you know the score. He gave more than his fair share. Didn't bitch about it then. Won't bitch now.

Ground Zero did a number on him. The chemicals, the dust, the silence in the pit. He doesn't remember what day it was when the coughing started, but it never really stopped.

Doctors gave him names for it. Alphabet soup diagnoses. But it all boiled down to the same thing: this job chewed him up.

And still, he shows up. Never forgets birthdays, funerals, podcasts, and late-night FaceTime with Evelyn's grandkids asking about Walt Disney World. He always looks forward to seeing friends over 50 years. Friends like John Byrne, Nancy McClurkin, Mike Kotarba, Marc Cowles, Joe Perla, and James Arslanian.

Roche is also grateful to 40-year friends like Herb Rutherford, Paul DeCotis, Rob Murphy, Sam Weitz, Ruben Gonzalez, Kevin Kozak, John Wells, and John Murray Neighbor Ernesto Clavijo for being there when help is needed.

You want to know who someone really is? Look at who still shows up after many years. These people didn't forget Toby when the badge came off. They didn't forget him when medical conditions showed up. They didn't scatter when things got heavy. They showed up with coffee, rides to appointments, stories from the old days, back when the job still made sense.

Guys like Murphy, DeCotis, Kozak, Gonzalez, Wells, Weitz, and Murray; they went way back. Back to when U.S. Customs was still Customs and the only "joint task force" was you and your partner in a beat-up Crown Vic or Chevy Impala. They laugh about the dumb things they did, the cases that went sideways, and the times they were focused on the goals.

Ernesto, the neighbor, is a retired local police executive officer. He's part of that rare breed, people who see someone hurting and step in without needing a reason. Other friends from the Florida Athletic Commission (Tim Devine, Jeff Thomas, to name a few) are always willing to help. That's the kind of loyalty you don't read about in policy manuals. That's the kind of inner circle the job builds.

Tobias is also grateful to Damaris Ramos Hernandez and Jeff Thomas, the Orlando connection. They have helped him greatly with an out the Miami area medical issue.

Finally, with the daily support of his ex-wife Aida Perez and his devoted daughter Marcy Roche, have made life easier for him. Several ex-colleagues from the Florida Joint Task Group (whom Roche recommended for a successful post-retirement employment) have completely turned their back on him when he needed help. Total disloyal scumbags. Also, several ex-friends from legacy Customs promised to help a family member but never came through. As Toby often says, "Later in life, you learn who you can count on!"

Aida could have walked away a long time ago. The job wrecked a lot of marriages. But even after the divorce, she stayed close. Helped him with the doctors. Managed paperwork. Made sure he remembered to eat, to rest, to slow down, things he never learned during his years chasing criminals.

Then there's Marcy. His daughter. His rock. The one who gets the full picture, scars, and all. She saw him broken. She saw him proud. She saw him torn up by regrets no one else could understand. But she stays close and visits. She showed up. She made it okay for him to display his true feelings. Marcy doesn't flinch when he talks about Ground Zero or the prison interviews, or the criminal justice life. She just listens. And sometimes, that's all a man like Toby needs.

Toby had the privilege and honor to host the podcast "Justice Then & Justice Now," created by him and FAC buddy Jeff Thomas. The guests had a unique perspective on the Criminal Justice System.

They were active participants, not media pundits or self-anointed experts. They were police officers, feds, attorneys, and former inmates. The podcast is on You Tube and social media, with over 5,000 friends on Facebook. The Real Deal.

Justice Now, Justice Then isn't some polished, corporate podcast with polished soundbites and sanitized narratives. It's raw. It and real. It's about war stories, redemption, and the kind of truth that gets edited out of DOJ press releases.

They brought on everyone, old-school narcotic cops, sharp-tongued defense attorneys, even lifers who did the time and lived to talk about it. No scripts. No filters. Just people who knew what the inside of a courtroom smells like.

Jeff Thomas and Tobias built the thing from scratch. Recorded in a renovated studio. Didn't matter. As long as the mics worked, the truth got told. And people listened. Toby gets messages now from rookies in law enforcement, retired homicide guys, and even ex-cons who say the podcast made them rethink life. That it mattered. That it felt honest. That's legacy. Not numbers. Not stats. Just the truth, one episode at a time.

In conclusion, Tobias feels that Paul Pelletier showed tremendous courage to fight through the disappointment. U.S. District Court Judge/Southern District of Florida Joan Lenard for showing the compassion for what the criminal justice system is based on. And Martha Romero for never giving up hope for her mother.

Finally award-winning Author Pete Thron, for telling the story correctly and accurately. Operation Evasion – The Ghost in You. He doesn't throw around praise lightly. But when he mentions Paul Pelletier, his voice changes. There's respect there, earned, not given. Pelletier didn't just talk tough. He stood tall when others folded. When it would've been easier to walk away, Paul doubled down. Stayed the course. That takes brass.

And Pete Thron, well, that's a different kind of gratitude. Because Pete didn't just author the story. He *got* it. He understood what it meant to carry this badge, this burden. He wrote it like a man who has walked through the fire and lived to bleed the truth on the page.

As for Judge Joan Lenard, Toby still remembers the look on her face during those decisive moments in court. She didn't grandstand. She didn't smirk like she was playing God. She listened.

She measured. And then she did what justice is supposed to do: *Balance the weight of the law, with the weight of the Soul.*

Martha Romero, the influence of the soul. She convinced Tobias Roche to take a second look at her mom (Evelyn Bozon Papa) and provided the roadmap to the success of the journey's end.

"Operation Evasion – The Ghost in You" wasn't a fairy tale. It was a resurrection. And Tobias Roche, ghosted, battered, but still standing, was proof that sometimes, the system stumbles its way into redemption.

"Inside you, the time moves, and she doesn't fade. The ghost in you, she doesn't fade."

I would like to personally thank Tobias Roche for giving me the opportunity to write about this incredible case and his stellar law enforcement career. And to Evelyn and Martha for never giving up hope...

THE END

www.ingramcontent.com/pod-product-compliance
Lightning Source LLC
LaVergne TN
LVHW021817060526
838201LV00058B/3419